Have you ever seen a seal? Seals have sleek fur and a thick layer of fat to help them keep warm when it is freezing.

Seals belong to the same family as dogs, but they don't have real legs, knees or feet so they are a bit clumsy on land. They have four flippers which they use to swim with.

There are two types of seals: seals that have ears, such as sea lions, and earless seals, such as the common seal.

Seals hunt at sea. They need to be speedy to catch the fish they eat. They also eat squid and shellfish and can swim 100m deep to reach them.

Seals live in the sea but breed on land, in bleak, windy places. Their pups stay on the beach till they can leave and swim away.

Seals take brief sleeps in the water, with their nose up so they can breathe.

A seal's whiskers help it to detect prey in the dim sea water. The hairs feel, 'see' and 'hear' which way to chase fish.

Fun fact! A group of dogs is a pack, a group of sheep is a flock. What is a group of seals? It is a bob or a pod.